TEENS FINANCIAL GUIDE

Money Wisdom For Modern Living

By
RICHARD R. Montemayor

Copyright

All right reserved. No part of this book Publication may be reproduced, distributed or transmitted in any form or by any means, including photocopying, recording, or other electronic or mechanical methods, without the prior permission of the publisher, except in the case of brief quotations embodied in critical reviews and certain other noncommercial uses permitted by copyright law.
Copyright © Richard R montemayor

Disclaimer

The information provided in this book, "Teen Financial Guide: Money Wisdom for Modern Living," is intended for educational purposes only. While every effort has been made to ensure the accuracy and reliability of the content, the author and publisher make no representations or warranties regarding the completeness, suitability, or applicability of the information presented.

Readers are advised to use their discretion and seek professional advice before making any financial decisions or taking any actions based on the information provided in this book.

The author and publisher disclaim any liability for any loss or damage arising directly or indirectly from the use of the information contained herein.

Furthermore, the views and opinions expressed in this book are those of the author and do not necessarily reflect the official policy or position of any organization or institution mentioned. Any references to specific products, services, companies, or organizations are for illustrative purposes only and do not constitute an endorsement or recommendation. Readers are encouraged to conduct their own research and consult with qualified professionals, such as financial advisors, accountants, or legal experts, to address their individual financial needs and circumstances.

By reading this book, readers acknowledge and agree to hold harmless the author, publisher, and any affiliated parties from any claims, damages, or losses arising from the use or reliance on the information provided in this book.

Your financial journey is unique, and while this book offers guidance and insights, ultimately, the responsibility for your financial decisions rests with you.

ACKNOWLEDGEMENT

As I reflect on the journey of creating "Teen Financial Guide: Money Wisdom for Modern Living," I am filled with gratitude for the many individuals who have contributed to its realization. First and foremost, I would like to express my deepest appreciation to the teens who inspired this book. Your curiosity, enthusiasm, and thirst for knowledge have been the driving force behind every chapter and concept. Your determination to take control of your financial futures is truly inspiring.

I am indebted to my family for their unwavering support and encouragement throughout this endeavor. Their belief in me and their willingness to lend a helping hand during the writing process is well appreciated.

To my mentors and advisors, thank you for sharing your expertise, insights, and guidance. Your wisdom and encouragement have enriched this book and shaped my understanding of personal finance.

I am grateful to the educators and professionals who contributed their knowledge and expertise to the content of this book. Your dedication to financial literacy and your commitment to empowering teens are commendable.

A special thank you to the readers of "Teen Financial Guide." Your interest in this book and your willingness to embark on this journey of financial empowerment are truly humbling. I hope that the knowledge and insights shared within these pages will serve as valuable tools on your path to financial success.

Finally, I would like to express my heartfelt gratitude to the entire team involved in the creation and publication of this book. From editors to designers, marketers to distributors, your collective efforts have brought "Teen Financial Guide" to life.

To all who have contributed to the realization of this book, thank you for your support, guidance, and encouragement. May "Teen Financial Guide" empower and inspire teens worldwide to embark on a journey of financial literacy, responsibility, and success.

With heartfelt appreciation,

Richard R. montemayor
CONTENT

Introduction: Navigating the Financial Landscape
- Understanding the Importance of Financial Literacy in Modern Times

Chapter 1: Foundations of Financial Wisdom
- Building a Strong Financial Mindset
- Setting Financial Goals for Success

Chapter 2: Earning and Managing Money
- Exploring Job Opportunities for Teens
- Budgeting Basics: Making Every Dollar Count

Chapter 3: Saving and Investing Strategies
- The Power of Saving: Starting Early for Future Success
- Introduction to Investing: Building Wealth for the Future

Chapter 4: Responsible Spending Habits
- Smart Shopping: Making Informed Purchases
- Avoiding Impulse Buys and Managing Peer Pressure

Chapter 5: Understanding Credit and Debt
- Demystifying Credit: The Good, the Bad, and the Ugly
- Managing Debt Wisely: Avoiding the Pitfalls of Overspending

Chapter 6: Planning for the Future
- Exploring Higher Education: Financial Considerations for College
- Looking Ahead: Building a Financially Secure Future
- Conclusion: Empowering Teens for Financial Independence**

INTRODUCTION

Navigating the financial Landscape

In our current reality where monetary entanglements and valuable open doors proliferate, understanding cash isn't simply an expertise , it's a superpower. Envision exploring the future with the certainty that you can deal with anything monetary difficulties come your direction. Imagine yourself graduating school obligation free, putting something aside for your most memorable vehicle, or in any event, going into business. These aren't simply dreams; they're totally inside your span. Furthermore, this book is here to direct you constantly.

For what reason is monetary proficiency so critical, particularly now? The response lies in the always advancing monetary scene of the 21st hundred years. The present economy is incomprehensibly unique in relation to that of your folks or grandparents. We're residing in a computerized age where cash can be made or lost with the snap of a button. Cryptographic money, web based banking, contributing applications , these are the new wildernesses of money, and dominating them can open entryways you never imagined.

Yet, here's the trick: without a strong comprehension of
how cash functions, these devices can become traps instead of entryways to progress. Visa obligation, rash spending, and monetary tricks are only a couple of the perils sitting tight for the ill-equipped. This book is intended to arm you with the information and systems to explore these difficulties and arise successfully.

All through these pages, you'll find functional exhortation on procuring, saving, spending, and putting away cash astutely. We'll jump into the quick and dirty of planning, the specialty of settling on savvy monetary choices, and the key to creating financial wellbeing from early on. This isn't simply an aide; it's your monetary playbook for present day living. Consider this book your own tutor, here to spur and motivate you. You'll find genuine accounts of teenagers who have changed their monetary prospects, alongside master tips custom fitted explicitly for your age bunch. We'll separate complex monetary ideas into straightforward language, ensuring you're furnished with the devices you really want to succeed.

Anyway, would you say you are prepared to open your monetary potential? Is it safe to say that you are ready to assume command over your cash and your future? *Teen Monetary Aide: Cash Insight for Present day Living* is something other than a book; it's your pass to independence from the rat race and a prosperous life. We should leave on this thrilling excursion together and transform your monetary dreams into the real world. What's to come is yours to shape, and it begins on the spot.

Understanding The Importance of Financial Literacy

Monetary education is the capacity to comprehend and actually utilize different monetary abilities, including individual monetary administration, planning, and money management. In the present speedy and always changing monetary scene, monetary proficiency has turned into a fundamental ability for everybody, especially for young people who are near the very edge of entering adulthood. Here is a top to bottom glance at why monetary education is critical in present day times.

1. Navigating Complex Monetary Systems

The monetary framework has become progressively mind boggling, with a plenty of items and administrations accessible to customers.

From Visas to educational loans, speculation records to retirement plans, understanding these choices and settling on informed choices requires a strong groundwork in monetary proficiency. Without this information, people are in danger of falling into obligation, settling on unfortunate venture decisions, or passing up chances to develop their abundance.

2. Preparing for the Future

The earlier people begin finding out about cash on the board, the more ready they will be for future monetary obligations. For teenagers, grasping the fundamentals of saving, effective money management, and planning can make way for a monetarily stable life. Monetary education helps in laying out sensible monetary objectives and conceiving procedures to accomplish them, whether it's putting something aside for school, purchasing a vehicle, or making arrangements for retirement.

3. Avoiding Obligation and Monetary Pitfalls

An absence of monetary information can prompt huge obligations and monetary pain. Youngsters who comprehend the ramifications of exorbitant financing costs on Mastercards and credits are better prepared to try not to amass obligation.

Financial education likewise implies finding out about the dangers related with different monetary items and the significance of living inside one's method.

4. Empowering Informed Choice Making

Monetary education engages people to make informed choices about their cash. This incorporates everything from ordinary spending to long haul ventures. By understanding ideas, for example, financing costs, expansion, and the time worth of cash, adolescents can go with decisions that will help them over the long haul. Informed direction likewise diminishes the probability of succumbing to monetary tricks and misrepresentation.

5. Enhancing Monetary Stability

On a more extensive scale, monetary proficiency adds to financial security and development. At the point when people are proficient about monetary administration, they are bound to save and contribute, which upholds the financial turn of events. Monetarily educated people are likewise more ready to climate monetary slumps and can add to a stronger economy.

6. Fostering Freedom and Responsibility

Monetary proficiency encourages a feeling of freedom and obligation. Adolescents who deal with their funds actually are less dependent on their folks and more fit for taking care of monetary difficulties all alone. This autonomy assembles certainty and furnishes youthful grown-ups with the abilities expected to explore the monetary parts of life.

7. Adapting to Mechanical Advances

The advanced monetary scene is intensely impacted by innovation. Computerized banking, online venture stages, and digital money are only a couple of instances of how innovation has changed finance. Monetary education helps teenagers comprehend and use these mechanical apparatuses for their potential benefit, they are not abandoned in an undeniably advanced world to guarantee them.

8. Promoting Monetary Prosperity and Stress Reduction

Monetary pressure is a huge issue for some people. By being monetarily educated, teenagers can keep away from a considerable lot of the stressors related to cash fumble. Understanding how to make a spending plan, save for crises, and contribute shrewdly can prompt a more noteworthy feeling of monetary security and generally speaking prosperity.

CHAPTER 1: Foundation of Financial Wisdom

Building a Strong Financial Mindset

Fostering areas of strength for an outlook is the foundation of making monetary progress and soundness. It goes past knowing how to spend, plan, save, and contribute; about developing mentalities and ways of behaving that support long haul monetary wellbeing. For youngsters, laying out a strong monetary mentality from the beginning can make them ready for a long period of savvy monetary choices. Here is a broad glance at how to fabricate areas of strength for a mentality.

1. Understanding the Worth of Money

The most vital phase in building areas of strength for a mentality is grasping the worth of cash. This includes perceiving that cash is a device that can assist with accomplishing objectives and work on personal satisfaction. It's tied in with having cash as well as about utilizing it shrewdly to set out open doors and secure your future.

To incorporate this, consider following your spending so that a month might be able to see where your cash goes and how it very well may be better used.

2. Setting Clear Monetary Goals

It is significant to Have clear monetary objectives. Objectives give guidance and inspiration. Begin by setting present moment, medium-term, and long haul monetary objectives. Transient objectives could incorporate putting something aside for another contraption, while medium-term objectives could include putting something aside for a vehicle or school. Long haul objectives could be tied in with building a just-in-case account or contributing for retirement. Record your objectives, make them explicit, and lay out a course of events for accomplishing them.

3. Cultivating Monetary Discipline

Monetary discipline is tied in with pursuing cognizant decisions that line up with your monetary objectives. This implies opposing the compulsion to make incautious buys and figuring out the significance of postponed satisfaction. Rehearsing discipline includes making and adhering to a financial plan, consistently inspecting your ways of managing money, and making changes depending on the situation. Instruments like planning applications can assist you with monitoring your funds and keep on track.

4. Developing an Investment funds Habit

Setting aside cash ought to turn into a non-debatable propensity. Indeed, even limited quantities saved routinely can collect over the long run and give monetary security.

Set up a framework where a piece of any cash you get, whether it's from a temporary work, remittance, or gifts, is naturally saved. Consider utilizing separate bank accounts for various objectives, for example, a backup stash, instruction, or a future vehicle acquisition.

5. Educating Yourself About Money

Information is power, particularly with regards to funds. Focus on consistently teaching yourself about individual budgets. Understand books, follow monetary websites, pay attention to digital recordings, and take online courses. Understanding ideas like accumulated dividends, the securities exchange, and retirement records can altogether affect your monetary choices and development.

6. Embracing a Development Mindset

A development mentality is the conviction that you can improve and develop through exertion and learning. When applied to funds, it implies seeing monetary slip-ups as learning valuable open doors as opposed to disappointments.

In the event that you overspend one month or make an unfortunate venture, dissect what turned out badly and how you can stay away from comparable errors later on. This outlook encourages flexibility and versatility, critical attributes for monetary achievement.

7. Practicing Appreciation and Contentment

Appreciation and happiness assume a critical part in monetary prosperity. Valuing what you have can diminish the inclination to pointlessly spend. Routinely rehearsing appreciation assists shift with centering from what you need to what you have, advancing a better relationship with cash. Satisfaction doesn't mean you ought to quit taking a stab at all the more yet rather tracking down a harmony among desire and appreciation.

8. Building Sound Monetary Habits

Creating sound monetary propensities is critical to keeping areas of strength for a mentality. Propensities, for example, routinely evaluating your spending plan, staying away from exorbitant premium obligation, shopping with a rundown, and correlation shopping can set aside cash and decrease monetary pressure. Computerizing reserve funds and bill installments can likewise guarantee consistency and forestall missed installments.

9. Seeking Monetary Exhortation and Mentorship

Make it a point to counsel from confided in sources. Guardians, instructors, or monetary consultants can offer significant experiences and direction. Finding a coach who has effectively explored their monetary excursion can furnish you with commonsense tips and support. Gaining from others' encounters can assist you with keeping away from normal entanglements and settling on informed choices.

10. Understanding the Effect of Way of life Choices

Your way of life decisions fundamentally influence your monetary wellbeing. This incorporates your ways of managing money, the sort of friendly exercises you participate in, and your utilization designs. Being aware of these decisions and their drawn out consequences for your funds is fundamental. Choosing a way of life that lines up with your monetary objectives instead of one driven by prevailing difficulties can prompt more prominent monetary dependability and fulfillment.

11. Balancing Chance and Reward
A solid monetary mentality implies figuring out the harmony among chance and prize. Teach yourself about various speculation choices and the related dangers. Enhancing your speculations can assist with overseeing risk and guarantee that you're not excessively presented to any single monetary item. Being OK with a specific degree of chance is essential for likely development, yet it ought to continuously be determined and informed.

Setting Financial Goals For Success

Laying out Financial objectives is a principal move toward making monetary progress. Objectives give guidance, inspiration, and a reasonable guide to monetary steadiness and development. For teenagers, laying out these objectives early can lay the basis for deep rooted monetary wellbeing. Here is a broad glance at how to define compelling monetary objectives for progress.

1. Understanding the Significance of Monetary Goals

Financial objectives are explicit goals you intend to accomplish with your cash. They assist you with remaining on track, focus on your spending, and measure your advancement.

Objectives likewise give a feeling of inspiration and inspiration, making it simpler to oppose enticements and settle on informed monetary choices. Understanding the reason why you really want monetary objectives is the most important phase in making and accomplishing them.

2. Different Sorts of Monetary Goals

Monetary objectives can be classified into three fundamental sorts: present moment, medium-term, and long haul. Each type fills an alternate need and requires an alternate methodology.

Transient Goals: These are objectives you intend to accomplish soon. Models incorporate putting something aside for another telephone, a unique occasion, or occasion gifts.

Momentary objectives are normally more modest and more quick.

Medium-Term Goals: These are objectives you plan to accomplish inside one to five years. They could incorporate putting something aside for a vehicle, an outing, or school costs. Medium-term objectives require really arranging and saving.

Long haul Goals: These objectives require over five years to accomplish and frequently incorporate significant achievements like purchasing a house, beginning a business, or retirement. Long haul objectives require predictable exertion and discipline over a lengthy period.

3. The Savvy Models for Setting Goals

Utilizing the Savvy models guarantees that your monetary objectives are clear cut and feasible. Shrewd represents Explicit, Quantifiable, Reachable, Important, and Time-bound.

Specific: Your objective ought to be clear and explicit. Rather than saying, "I need to set aside cash," determine the sum and reason, similar to "I need to save $500 for another PC."

Measurable: You ought to have the option to keep tabs on your development. Set quantifiable benchmarks, for example, saving $50 every month.

Achievable: Your objective ought to be sensible and feasible in view of your ongoing monetary circumstance. Consider your pay and costs to lay out a functional objective.

Relevant: Guarantee your objective lines up with your more extensive life plans and monetary targets. Putting something aside for school is pertinent on the off chance that you intend to seek after advanced education.

Time-bound: Set a cutoff time for accomplishing your objective. This makes a need to keep moving and assists you with remaining focused. For instance, "I need to save $500 for another PC by December."

4. Steps to Setting Monetary Goals

To define compelling monetary objectives, follow these means:

1. Assess Your Current Monetary Situation: Grasp your pay, costs, obligations, and investment funds. This evaluation distinguishes regions where you can improve and lay out sensible objectives.

2. Identify Your Priorities: Figure out what means quite a bit to you. Is it putting something aside for instruction, purchasing a vehicle, or building a secret stash? Focus on your objectives in light of your necessities and values.

3. Break Down Objectives into Significant Steps: Separation of bigger objectives into more modest, reasonable advances. For example, in the event that you want to save $1,200 for an excursion in a year, plan to save $100 every month.

4. Create a Budget: A spending plan assists you with designating your pay toward your objectives. Track your spending and recognize regions where you can scale back to save more.

5. Set Up Programmed Savings: Computerize your reserve funds to guarantee consistency. Set up programmed moves to your bank account to make saving simpler and more reliable.

6. Monitor Your Progress: Routinely audit your advancement toward your objectives. Change your financial plan and saving techniques depending on the situation to keep focused.

7. Celebrate Milestones: Perceive and celebrate when you arrive at achievements en route. This keeps you spurred and supports a positive monetary way of behaving.

5. Overcoming Normal Challenges

Putting forth and accomplishing monetary objectives can accompany difficulties. This is the way to beat normal impediments:

Absence of Motivation: Stay inspired by picturing the advantages of arriving at your objectives. Keep tokens of your objectives apparent and celebrate little wins.

Surprising Expenses: Fabricate a secret stash to cover unanticipated costs without crashing your objectives. Intend to save three to a half a year of everyday costs.

Hasty Spending: Practice discretion and care with spending. Prior to making a buy, inquire as to whether it lines up with your monetary objectives.

Peer Pressure: Stay consistent with your monetary needs notwithstanding friendly impacts. Encircle yourself with strong companions who regard your objectives.

6. The Job of Monetary Education

Teaching yourself about individual budgets is pivotal for defining and accomplishing monetary objectives. Find out about planning, saving, financial planning, and obligation to the board. The more educated you are, the better prepared you'll be to settle on shrewd monetary choices. Use assets like books, online courses, and monetary applications to upgrade your insight.

7. The Advantages of Monetary Goals

Putting forth monetary objectives offers various advantages:

Upgraded Monetary Security: Objectives assist you with building investment funds, pay off past

commitments, and plan for unforeseen costs.
Worked on Monetary Discipline: Making progress toward objectives imparts discipline and energizes savvy monetary propensities.
More prominent Monetary Freedom: Accomplishing objectives gives more opportunity to seek after open doors and encounters without monetary pressure.
Feeling of Accomplishment: Arriving at your objectives gives pride and lifts your trust in overseeing cash.

CHAPTER 2: EARNING AND MANAGING MONEY

Exploring Job Opportunities For Teens

For teens, investigating open positions is something other than making additional money. It's tied in with acquiring important experience, growing new abilities, and building an establishment for future vocation achievement. Securing the right position can likewise impart a feeling of obligation, hard working attitude, and monetary freedom. Here is a broad aide on investigating open positions for teenagers, including the advantages, sorts of occupations, how to track them down, and tips for progress.

1. Benefits of Filling in as a Teen

Filling in as a youngster offers various advantages past the check:

Monetary Independence: Bringing in your own cash gives a feeling of freedom and the capacity to put something aside for individual objectives, like purchasing a vehicle, putting something aside for school, or financing leisure activities.

Work Experience: Early work experience is significant. It shows you how to collaborate in an expert climate, oversee time really, and foster areas of strength for an ethic.

Expertise Development: Various positions assist with creating different abilities, for example, correspondence, critical thinking, collaboration, and client support. These abilities are adaptable and helpful in ongoing vocations.

Continue Building: Having work insight on your resume makes you more alluring to future bosses and school affirmations officials. It shows that you are mindful and equipped for offsetting work with different responsibilities.

Networking: Occupations furnish potential chances to meet and associate with experts who can offer direction, mentorship, and references for future open doors.

2. Types of Occupations for Teens

Teenagers can investigate an assortment of open positions across various enterprises. Here are some normal work types appropriate for young people:

Retail and Client Service: Working in retail locations, supermarkets, or drive-through joints gives insight in client support, cash taking care of, and cooperation.

Looking after children

Childcare: Watching adaptable hours and the opportunity to foster liability and providing care abilities.

Tutoring: In the event that you succeed in a specific subject, coaching peers or more youthful understudies can be a compensating method for bringing in cash and supporting your insight.

Pet Sitting and Canine Walking: For creature darlings, pet sitting and canine strolling offer adaptable, charming work.

Yard Care and Landscaping: Occasional positions like cutting yards, raking leaves, or scooping snow give actual work and a feeling of achievement.

Entry level positions and Apprenticeships: A few enterprises offer temporary jobs or apprenticeships to teenagers, giving active involvement with fields like tech, media, or exchanges.

Independent and Online Jobs: With the ascent of the gig economy, adolescents can investigate independent open doors like visual communication, composing, web-based entertainment the executives, or virtual help.

Camp Counselor: Filling in as a camp guide throughout the mid year

can be tomfoolery and creates authority and relational abilities.
Lifeguard: For those with solid swimming abilities, turning into a lifeguard at a neighborhood pool or ocean side can be remunerating summer work.

3. How to Secure Position Opportunities

Getting a new line of work as a youngster requires some work and genius. Here are moves toward assist you with beginning:
Influence Individual Networks: Ask family, companions, instructors, and neighbors assuming that they are aware of any employment opportunities. Individual proposals can frequently prompt open positions.
Visit Neighborhood Businesses: Approach nearby organizations straightforwardly and ask about employment opportunities. Bring a resume and be ready to finish up an application on the spot.
Utilize Online Work Portals: Sites like For sure, Snagajob, and neighborhood local area loads up frequently list temporary positions appropriate for youngsters. A few organizations likewise have committed pages for understudying open positions.
Check School Resources: Many schools have vocation focuses or worksheets that post neighborhood employment opportunities for understudies. School instructors can likewise offer direction.
Investigate Volunteer Opportunities: Chipping in can here and there prompt paid positions. It's

an extraordinary method for acquiring experience, fabricating an organization, and showing your responsibility and hard working attitude.

Use Social Media: Follow neighborhood organizations and local area pages via online entertainment stages. Managers frequently post employment opportunities on their virtual entertainment profiles.

Go to Occupation Fairs: Search for neighborhood work fairs, particularly those focused on youngsters and understudies. These occasions can give direct admittance to bosses hoping to employ teenagers.

4. Tips for Occupation Success

Whenever you've gotten some work, it is essential to succeed in your job. Here are a few hints to assist you with succeeding:

Be Dependable and Reliable: Generally show up on time and be trustworthy. Consistency assembles trust and exhibits your responsibility.

Keep a Positive Attitude: Approach your occupation with energy and a readiness to learn. An inspirational perspective can separate you and make you an esteemed worker.

Impart Effectively: Clear correspondence with your manager and associates is fundamental. Go ahead and ask questions in the event that you're uncertain about something.

Be Professional: Dress suitably for your work, follow the organization's set of principles, and keep an expert disposition.

Oversee Time Wisely: Offsetting work with school and different obligations calls for great use of time productively. Utilize an organizer or computerized schedule to monitor your timetable.

Look for Feedback: Routinely request criticism from your manager to grasp your assets and regions for development. Utilize this input to develop and improve your presentation.

Show Initiative: Search for chances to blow away your expected set of responsibilities. Demonstrating energy can prompt extra liabilities and amazing open doors for headway.

Assemble Relationships: Foster positive associations with your partners and bosses. Organizing inside your occupation can prompt future open doors and important references.

5. Legal Contemplations and Working Hours

Adolescents ought to know about the legitimate parts of working, including work regulations that administer youth business. These regulations differ by nation and state yet for the most part include:

Work Permits: A few spots expect teenagers to get a work grant prior to beginning some work.

Working Hours: There are limitations on the quantity of hours teenagers can work, particularly during the school year. For instance, in the U.S., 14-and 15-year-olds can stir as long as 3 hours on a school day and 18 hours in a school week.

Least Wage: Adolescents are qualified for essentially the lowest pay permitted by law, despite the fact that it might contrast for more youthful specialists.

Dangerous Jobs: There are limitations on the kinds of positions adolescents can perform, particularly those considered risky.

Understanding these guidelines guarantees that youngsters are safeguarded.

Budgeting Basics: Making Every Dollar Count

Planning is a major monetary expertise that assists you with dealing with your cash really, guaranteeing that each dollar you procure is effectively utilized. For teenagers, figuring out how to spend money early sets the establishment for monetary autonomy and progress in adulthood.

1. Understanding the Significance of Budgeting

Planning is fundamental because of multiple factors:

Monetary Control: A financial plan gives you command over your funds, permitting you to settle on informed conclusions about how to spend and save.

Objective Achievement: Planning helps you put forth and accomplish monetary objectives, whether it's putting something aside for a major buy, financing a side interest, or making arrangements for school.

Keeping away from Debt: By following your pay and costs, a spending plan assists you with trying

not to overspend and collecting obligations.
Building Savings: A financial plan urges you to save routinely, making a wellbeing net for crises and future necessities.
Decreasing Stress: Knowing precisely where your cash goes can lessen monetary pressure and tension.

2. Steps to Make a Budget
Making a financial plan includes a few key stages. Here is a nitty gritty manual for assist you with getting everything rolling:
Stage 1: Ascertain Your Pay
Start by deciding your all out month to month pay. This incorporates:
Profit from Jobs: Incorporate wages from temporary positions, temporary jobs, or independent work.
Allowances: On the off chance that you get a customary stipend from your folks, incorporate this sum.
Gifts and Bonuses: Any money related gifts or rewards ought to likewise be figured in.
Your pay is the beginning stage of your spending plan, providing you with a reasonable image of the amount of cash you possess to work with every month.
Stage 2: Rundown Your Costs
Then, list all your month to month expenses. These can be separated into fixed and variable costs:
Fixed Expenses: These are customary, reliable expenses, for example,
Transportation: Transport charge, gas, or vehicle support.

Telephone Bill: Regularly scheduled installments for your cell phone.
Subscriptions: Web-based features, gaming participations, or different memberships.
Variable Expenses: These change every month and include:
Food: Eating out, snacks, or snacks at school.
Entertainment: Motion pictures, shows, or other relaxation exercises.
Clothing: New garments or embellishments.
Individual Care: Hair styles, toiletries, or excellence items.
Following your costs assists you with understanding where your cash proceeds to distinguish regions where you can scale back if necessary.
Stage 3: Put forth Monetary Objectives
Recognize your present moment and long haul monetary objectives. Models include:
Momentary Goals: Putting something aside for another telephone, an extraordinary occasion, or a show.
Long haul Goals: Putting something aside for a vehicle, schooling cost, or a backup stash.
Setting clear, attainable objectives gives inspiration and bearing to your planning endeavors.
Stage 4: Plan Your Financial plan
With your pay and costs recorded and your objectives at the top of the priority list, now is the right time to make your spending plan. Dispense bits of your pay to cover your costs and reserve funds. A basic planning strategy is the 50/30/20 rule:

half for Needs: Assign half of your pay to fundamental costs like transportation, food, and telephone bills.
30% for Wants: Utilize 30% for unnecessary costs like amusement and leisure activities.
20% for Savings: Devote 20% of your pay to investment funds and monetary objectives.
Change these rates in light of your own conditions and monetary needs.
Stage 5: Track and Change Your Spending plan
Routinely track your spending to guarantee you're adhering to your financial plan. Use planning applications, bookkeeping sheets, or a diary to record your pay and costs. Toward the finish of every month, audit your financial plan:
Contrast Genuine Enjoying with Your Budget: Recognize regions where you overspent or underspent.
Change as Needed: Make essential acclimations to remain focused. On the off chance that you overspend in one classification, search for ways of scaling back in another.
3. Tips for Powerful Budgeting
To put forth your planning attempts more powerful, think about these tips:
Be Realistic: Draw sensible spending lines and investment funds objectives in light of your pay and costs.
Focus on Savings: Treat reserve funds as a decent cost. Mechanize moves to your bank account to guarantee consistency.
Track Each Expense: Record every one of your costs, regardless of how

little. Little buys can add up and affect your financial plan.

Stay away from Motivation Purchases: Prior to making a buy, inquire as to whether it's a need or a need. Postpone unimportant buys to stay away from rash spending.

Survey Regularly: Routinely audit and update your financial plan to reflect changes in your pay or costs.

Remain Flexible: Life is capricious, and your spending plan ought to be sufficiently adaptable to oblige surprising costs or changes in your monetary circumstance.

Use Planning Tools: Use planning applications like Mint, YNAB (You Want A Spending plan), or a straightforward calculation sheet to really follow your pay and costs.

4. Common Planning Difficulties and How to Defeat Them

Planning can accompany difficulties, particularly while you're beginning. Here are normal hindrances and how to beat them:

Conflicting Income: Assuming your pay changes from one month to another, base your spending plan on your normal pay. Save extra in major league salary months to cover shortages in low-pay months.

Unforeseen Expenses: Fabricate a backup stash to cover surprising costs like vehicle fixes or doctor's visit expenses. Mean to save something like three to a half year of everyday costs.

Adhering to the Budget: Assuming you find it hard to adhere to your financial plan, survey your ways of managing money and recognize triggers for overspending. Change your spending plan to be more sensible and obliging.

Absence of Motivation: Stay roused by setting clear, attainable objectives and remunerating yourself for arriving at achievements. Envision the advantages of accomplishing your monetary objectives to remain on track.

5. The Job of Reserve funds in Budgeting

Saving is a basic part of planning. This is the way to really consolidate investment funds:

Crisis Fund: Focus on building a backup stash for unexpected costs. This gives monetary security and true serenity.

Explicit Goals: Put something aside for explicit objectives, like purchasing another device, going out traveling, or financing a side interest. Having an unmistakable reason for your investment funds makes it more straightforward to remain committed.

Long haul Savings: Consider long haul reserve funds for tremendous costs like schooling cost, a vehicle, or even a future home. Begin ahead of schedule to profit from accumulating interest.

Investment funds Accounts: Utilize separate investment accounts for various objectives. This assists you with keeping tabs on your development and remaining coordinated.

CHAPTER 3: SAVING AND INVESTING STRATEGIES

The power of Saving: Starting Early for Future Success

Setting aside cash is a foundation of monetary strength and achievement. The prior you start, the more you can use the force of self multiplying dividends, foster restrained monetary propensities, and make a safe future. For youngsters, understanding and embracing the act of saving can make way for deep rooted monetary wellbeing.

1. The Significance of Saving Early

Beginning to set aside cash right off the bat in life enjoys various benefits:

Build Interest: One of the most convincing motivations to save early is to accumulate interest. Here the cash you save acquires revenue, and that premium procures revenue over the long haul. The prior you begin saving, the additional time your cash needs to dramatically develop.

Monetary Security: Having reserve funds gives a monetary pad that can safeguard you in the midst of crisis, for example, surprising doctor's visit expenses, vehicle fixes, or employment misfortune.

Objective Achievement: Investment funds empower you to arrive at your monetary objectives, whether it's purchasing a vehicle, subsidizing your schooling, or voyaging.

Obligation Avoidance: By putting something aside for future costs, you can abstain from depending on using a credit card and collecting obligation, which frequently accompanies exorbitant loan fees and can be trying to pay off.

Monetary Independence: Early reserve funds can prompt more noteworthy monetary autonomy and opportunity, permitting you to settle on decisions that line up with your qualities and objectives without being compelled by monetary limits.

2. Understanding Compound Interest

To get a handle on the force of saving early, it's fundamental to comprehend how self multiplying dividends functions. Here is an essential clarification:

Straightforward Interest versus Build Interest: Straightforward interest is determined exclusively on the underlying sum, though accumulated interest is determined on the importance in addition to any collected interest. This implies your cash becomes quicker with build revenue.

The Equation for Build Interest: The equation for accumulate interest is $A = P(1 + r/n)^{(nt)}$, where:

An is how much cash gathered after a year, including revenue.

P is the chief sum

r is the yearly financing cost

n is the time interest it accumulated each year.

t is the quantity of years the cash is contributed.

For instance, assuming you save $1,000 at a yearly loan cost of 5%, accumulated every year, following 10 years, you would have roughly $1,628.89. The prior you start, the more critical the effect of progressive accrual.

3. Setting Reserve funds Goals

To capitalize on your reserve funds, defining clear and feasible goals is critical. This is the way to make it happen:

transient Goals: These are objectives you plan to accomplish in the span of a little while. Models incorporate putting something aside for another telephone, a gaming console, or an extraordinary occasion.

Medium-Term Goals: These objectives are set for a time period of one to five years. They could incorporate putting something aside for a vehicle, a huge outing, or school costs.

Long haul Goals: These are objectives that require over five years to accomplish, like putting something aside for an initial investment on a house, retirement, or going into business.

Having explicit investment funds objectives gives guidance and inspiration. Record your objectives, decide the amount you want to save, and set a timetable for accomplishing them.

4. Strategies for Compelling Saving

Executing compelling saving methodologies guarantees that you keep focused and arrive at your monetary objectives. Here are a few key methodologies:

Pay Yourself First: Deal with your reserve funds like a bill that should be paid consistently. Distribute a piece of your pay to investment funds prior to spending on anything more.

Computerize Your Savings: Set up programmed moves from your financial records to your investment account. This guarantees consistency and eliminates the compulsion to spend the cash.

Make a Budget: A spending plan assists you with following your pay and costs, recognize regions where you can scale back, and distribute more cash to investment funds.

Use Investment accounts with Exorbitant Premium Rates: Search for bank accounts that offer higher financing costs to augment the development of your reserve funds. Consider choices like high return investment accounts or authentications of stores.

Live Beneath Your Means: Stay away from way of life expansion by holding your spending under tight restraints as your pay increases. Center around needs versus needs and focus on saving over superfluous spending.

Track Your Progress: Routinely survey your investment funds objectives and keep tabs on your development. Change your systems on a case by case basis to keep on track.

5. Overcoming Normal Saving Challenges

Setting aside cash can be testing, particularly with contending monetary needs and enticements. This is the way to conquer normal impediments:

Drive Spending: Make a holding up period prior to making huge buys. This assists you with keeping away from hasty choices and guarantees that you're spending on things that genuinely matter.

Peer Pressure: Stay consistent with your monetary objectives notwithstanding prevalent difficulties to spend. Encircle yourself with companions who regard your monetary decisions and offer comparative qualities.

Absence of Income: On the off chance that your pay is restricted, search for ways of expanding it, for example, requiring on a section investment work, outsourcing, or selling things you never again need.

Surprising Expenses: Assemble a secret stash to take care of unforeseen expenses. This asset goes about as a monetary support, permitting you to keep putting something aside for your objectives without disturbance.

Procrastination: Begin saving currently, regardless of whether it's a modest quantity. The propensity for saving is a higher priority than the sum you save at first. Increment your reserve funds over the long run as your pay develops.

6. The Job of Monetary Education

Understanding individual accounting is basic to compelling saving. Monetary instruction engages you to go with informed choices and keep away from normal traps. Here are far to upgrade your monetary information:

Understand Books and Articles: There are various books and online assets committed to individual budgets. A few famous titles incorporate "The All out Cash Makeover" by Dave Ramsey and "Rich Father Unfortunate Father" by Robert Kiyosaki.

Take Online Courses: Stages like Coursera, Khan Institute, and Udemy offer seminars on planning, money management, and monetary preparation.

Follow Monetary Sites and Podcasts: Stay refreshed with the most recent monetary tips and patterns by following legitimate monetary online journals and paying attention to back related digital recordings.

Gain from Mentors: Look for exhortation from guardians, instructors, or monetary counselors who can give direction and offer their encounters.

7. The Advantages of Long haul Saving

The advantages of beginning to save early stretch out a long way past quick monetary security. Here are a few long haul benefits:

Monetary Freedom: Long haul reserve funds give the opportunity to settle on important decisions without being compelled by monetary concerns.

This incorporates voyaging, chasing after advanced education, or beginning a business.
Retirement Planning: Beginning a retirement reserve early guarantees an agreeable and secure retirement. The force of accruing funds implies that even little commitments can develop essentially after some time.
Major Purchases: Saving early assists you with managing the cost of huge life costs, like purchasing a home, subsidizing your kids' schooling, or buying a vehicle without depending on credits.
Stress Reduction: Monetary dependability diminishes pressure and uneasiness, permitting you to zero in on self-improvement, connections, and profession advancement.

Introduction to Investing: Building Wealth For the Future

Contributing is an incredible asset for creating financial momentum and accomplishing long haul monetary objectives. Dissimilar to saving, which regularly includes saving cash in an okay record, putting includes placing your cash into resources like stocks, securities, or land that can possibly develop over the long haul. For teenagers and youthful grown-ups, beginning to contribute early can be especially valuable because of the drawn out development potential and the force of self multiplying dividends.

1. Understanding the Significance of Investing

Contributing is fundamental because of multiple factors:

Abundance Accumulation: Putting away permits your cash to develop over the long run, possibly giving a better yield than a standard investment account.

Beating Inflation: Ventures can assist you with outperforming expansion, which disintegrates the buying influence of cash over the long run. By acquiring returns that surpass the expansion rate, your cash holds its worth.

Accomplishing Monetary Goals: Contributing can assist you with accomplishing critical monetary objectives like purchasing a house, subsidizing schooling, beginning a business, or getting a familiar retirement.

Monetary Security: A differentiated speculation portfolio can give monetary security and steadiness, shielding you from financial vacillations and vulnerabilities.

2. Types of Investments

There are different kinds of speculations, each with its own gamble and bring profile back. Here is a gander at some normal speculation choices:

Stocks

Definition: Stocks address possession partakes in an organization. At the point when you purchase stocks, you become an investor and can profit from the organization's development and benefit.

Returns: Stocks have the potential for exceptional yields through capital appreciation and profits.
Risk: Stocks are unstable and can change in esteem. The gamble is higher contrasted with securities and investment accounts, however the potential returns are likewise more prominent.

Bonds
Definition: Bonds are obligation protections given by enterprises or legislatures. At the point when you purchase a security, you are basically loaning cash to the backer in return for occasional premium installments and the arrival of the chief sum at development.
Returns: Bonds offer fixed returns as revenue installments, making them a more steady speculation.
Risk: Bonds are for the most part safer than stocks yet at the same time convey gambles, particularly assuming the guarantor defaults.

Shared Funds
Definition: Shared finances pool cash from numerous financial backers to purchase a differentiated arrangement of stocks, bonds, or different protections. They are overseen by proficient asset directors.
Returns: Returns rely upon the exhibition of the basic resources. Common assets give expansion, lessening risk.
Risk: The gamble fluctuates in light of the asset's venture technique. A few assets are more moderate, while others are forceful.

Trade Exchanged Assets (ETFs)

Definition: ETFs are like shared reserves yet are exchanged on stock trades like individual stocks. They intend to repeat the presentation of a particular file, area, or item.
Returns: ETFs offer returns in view of the exhibition of the record or area they track.
Risk: ETFs convey market risk, like stocks, however offer broadening like shared reserves.

Genuine Estate
Definition: Putting resources into land includes buying property like private, business, or investment properties.
Returns: Returns come from rental pay and property estimation appreciation.
Risk: Land requires huge capital and conveys dangers, for example, market vacillations, support expenses, and property the board difficulties.

Cryptocurrencies
Definition: Digital forms of money are advanced or virtual monetary standards that utilize cryptography for security. Bitcoin and Ethereum are well known models.
Returns: Digital forms of money can offer significant yields because of their instability.
Risk: They are profoundly speculative and unstable, with the potential for critical misfortunes.

3. Principles of Investing
Understanding key standards can assist you with settling on informed venture choices:

Begin Early
Force of Compounding: The earlier you begin money management, the more you can profit from building

revenue, where your income creates extra profit over the long haul. This remarkable development can altogether build your riches.

Diversification

Risk Management: Expanding your speculations across various resource classes (stocks, bonds, land) and areas decreases risk. On the off chance that one venture performs ineffectively, others might perform well, adjusting your general portfolio.

Risk Tolerance

Surveying Risk: Comprehend your gamble resilience, which is your capacity and ability to get through market instability and likely misfortunes. More youthful financial backers can regularly stand to face more challenges because of a more extended venture skyline.

Long haul Perspective

Staying away from Market Timing: Contributing with a drawn out viewpoint assists you with keeping fixed on your objectives and keeping away from the traps of attempting to time the market, which is famously troublesome and dangerous.

Research and Due Diligence

Informed Decisions: Lead intensive exploration prior to settling on speculation choices. Comprehend the basics of the speculations you pick and remain informed about market patterns and monetary circumstances.

4. Steps to Begin Investing

Here is a bit by bit manual for assist you with starting your speculation process:

Stage 1: Instruct Yourself

Learning Resources: Read books, take online courses, and follow monetary news to fabricate your insight about effective money management. A few suggested books incorporate "The Smart Financial backer" by Benjamin Graham and "Rich Father Unfortunate Father" by Robert Kiyosaki.

Stage 2: Set Monetary Goals

Clear Objectives: Characterize your monetary objectives, like putting something aside for school, purchasing a house, or retirement. Clear objectives assist you with picking the right speculations and remain persuaded.

Stage 3: Survey Your Monetary Situation

Planning and Saving: Guarantee you have a strong spending plan and investment funds plan. Fabricate a secret stash with three to a half year of everyday costs before you begin effective financial planning.

Stage 4: Pick a Speculation Account

Business Accounts: Open a money market fund with a legitimate firm. Consider factors like charges, account types, and speculation choices. For long haul objectives, consider charge advantaged accounts like IRAs or 401(k)s.

Stage 5: Foster a Speculation Strategy

Resource Allocation: Settle on a resource portion that lines up with your gamble resilience and monetary objectives. For instance, a youthful financial backer could pick a higher

distribution of stocks for development potential.
Normal Contributions: Contribute routinely, like month to month commitments, to profit from mitigating risk over the long term, which decreases the effect of market unpredictability.

Stage 6: Screen and Change Your Portfolio

Occasional Review: Consistently survey your ventures and portfolio execution. Rebalance your portfolio on a case by case basis to keep up with your ideal resource distribution.
Remain Informed: Stay aware of market patterns, monetary pointers, and changes in your own monetary circumstance.

5. Common Venture Errors to Avoid

To expand your odds of coming out on top, know about normal venture botches:
Absence of Diversification: Don't place all your cash into one speculation. Broaden to spread risk.
Profound Investing: Try not to settle on speculation choices in view of feelings like apprehension or eagerness. Adhere to your drawn out methodology.
Disregarding Fees: Be aware of charges and costs, as they can eat into your profits over the long haul.
Pursuing Performance: Don't pursue the most recent hot stock or pattern. Center around strong, long haul speculations.
Disregarding Research: Generally direct intensive examination prior to financial planning. Grasp the dangers and possible returns.

CHAPTER 4
RESPONSIBLE SHOPPING

Smart Shopping : Making Informed Purchases

Smart shopping includes pursuing informed choices while buying labor and products, guaranteeing that you get the best incentive for your cash. Whether you're purchasing food, garments, hardware, or whatever else, being a smart customer can set aside your cash, time, and disappointment. Here is a broad aide on brilliant shopping and how to make informed buys.

1. Understanding the Significance of Brilliant Shopping

Smart shopping is fundamental because of multiple factors:

Saving Money: Making informed buys assists you with setting aside cash by tracking down the best arrangements, keeping away from superfluous costs, and boosting the worth of your buys.

Quality Assurance: Shrewd shopping guarantees that you purchase great items that address your issues and assumptions, diminishing the gamble of disappointment or lament.

Time Efficiency: By exploring items and looking at costs in advance, you can smooth out the shopping system and abstain from throwing away energy on superfluous perusing or hasty purchases.

Natural Impact: Going with cognizant buying choices, like purchasing from maintainable brands or picking eco-accommodating items, can add to natural protection and diminish squander.

Empowerment: Brilliant shopping enables you as a shopper, permitting you to pursue informed decisions that line up with your qualities, inclinations, and spending plan.

2. Steps to Savvy Shopping

Follow these moves toward become a brilliant customer and make informed buys:

Stage 1: Exploration Items

Prior to making a buy, research the item completely. Think about elements like quality, highlights, particulars, and audits from different purchasers. Utilize dependable sources, for example, buyer reports, item survey sites, and client discussions to accumulate data.

Stage 2: Think about Costs

Contrast costs from various retailers with guarantee you're getting the best arrangement. Search for limits, advancements, and deals to boost investment funds. Online cost correlation instruments and program expansions can assist you with rapidly looking at costs across numerous retailers.

Stage 3: Really look at Merchandise exchanges and Guarantees

Prior to making a buy, survey the retailer's merchandise exchange and guarantee terms. Guarantee that you grasp the circumstances for returns,

trades, and discounts on the off chance that the item doesn't live up to your assumptions or has deserts.
Stage 4: Think about Worth Over Cost
While cost is significant, think about the general worth of the item. Factors like sturdiness, unwavering quality, execution, and client service add to the item's incentive. In some cases, following through on a greater expense forthright for a quality item can set aside your cash over the long haul.
Stage 5: Assess Long haul Expenses
While contrasting items, consider long haul expenses like upkeep, fixes, and working costs. A less expensive item might have higher long haul costs in the event that it requires successive fixes or consumes more energy.
Stage 6: Search for Limits and Rewards
Exploit limits, coupons, steadfastness programs, and cashback offers to get a good deal on your buys. Pursue retailer bulletins and follow them via web-based entertainment to remain informed about selective arrangements and advancements.
Stage 7: Read the Fine Print
Painstakingly read item depictions, agreements, and guarantee data prior to making a buy. Focus on secret expenses, transporting costs, and any limitations or restrictions that might apply.
3. Tips for Brilliant Shopping
Set a Budget: Decide the amount you're willing to spend prior to shopping and adhere to your financial plan to abstain from overspending.

Focus on Needs Over Wants: Separate between fundamental buys and optional spending. Center around satisfying your requirements first prior to enjoying quite a while.

Stay away from Motivation Buying: Take as much time as is needed to consider buys cautiously and try not to pursue incautious choices. Interruption and think prior to making a buy, particularly for superfluous things.

Shop Off-Season: Exploit slow time of year deals and freedom occasions to score extraordinary arrangements on occasional things like apparel, hardware, and outside gear.

Purchase in Bulk: Think about purchasing things in mass or bigger amounts on the off chance that it appears to be legit and assuming you'll utilize them routinely. This can frequently bring about huge reserve funds per unit.

Arrange Prices: Feel free to arrange costs, particularly for expensive things or while purchasing from autonomous merchants. You might have the option to get a lower cost or extra advantages by arranging.

Check for Item Recalls: Prior to buying items, check for any reviews or security alerts given by the maker or pertinent specialists. Try not to buy reviewed items to guarantee your security and fulfillment.

4. Staying Protected While Shopping

Shop from Trustworthy Retailers: Stick to notable, respectable retailers with a background marked by certain client surveys and dependable client support.

Utilize Secure Installment Methods: While making on the web buys, utilize secure installment techniques, for example, Visas or trustworthy installment passages that offer purchaser assurance.

Safeguard Individual Information: Be mindful about sharing individual and monetary data on the web. Just furnish touchy data on secure sites with HTTPS encryption.

5. The Job of Innovation in Brilliant Shopping

Value Correlation Tools: Use cost examination sites and applications to think about costs from different retailers and find the best arrangements rapidly.

Cashback and Prizes Apps: Exploit cashback and rewards applications that proposition refunds, limits, and steadfastness focuses for shopping at partaking retailers.

Coupon and Markdown Apps: Use coupon and rebate applications to track down advanced coupons, promotion codes, and selective arrangements for on the web and in-store buys.

Program Extensions: Introduce program augmentations that consequently apply coupon codes and limits at checkout, setting aside your time and cash.

Avoiding Impulse Buys and Managing Peer Pressure

Keeping away from spur of the moment purchases and overseeing peer pressure are significant abilities for youngsters to create as they explore the universe of industrialism and social connections. Hasty purchases can prompt superfluous spending and monetary pressure, while peer strain can impact youngsters to pursue choices that may not line up with their qualities or monetary objectives.

Keeping away from Hasty purchases

1. Identify Triggers: Perceive circumstances or feelings that trigger spur of the moment purchases, like weariness, stress, or social impact. By understanding your triggers, you can foster procedures to actually address them.

2. Create a Shopping List: Prior to going out to shop, make a rundown of things you really want to buy and adhere to it. This assists you with remaining on track and abstain from being influenced by enticing showcases or advancements.

3. Set Spending Limits: Lay out spending limits for optional buys and stick to them. Consider utilizing cash rather than Visas for optional spending to forestall overspending.

4. Delay Gratification: Work on postponing delight by holding up 24 hours prior to making trivial buys. This permits time to drive desires to die down and assists you with settling on additional smart choices.

5. Avoid Shopping When Emotional: Shun shopping while you're feeling personal or powerless, as you're bound to make spur of the moment purchases to satisfy brief feelings.

6. Shop with Purpose: While shopping, center around satisfying explicit requirements as opposed to perusing erratically. Try not to meander around stores or online stages without a reasonable reason.

7. Practice Contentment: Develop an outlook of satisfaction and appreciation for what you as of now have. Help yourself to remember the worth of encounters and connections over material belongings.

Overseeing Companion Tension

1. Know Your Values: Explain your own qualities, needs, and monetary objectives. When confronted with peer strain to spend, help yourself to remember what makes the biggest difference to you and settle on choices lined up with your qualities.

2. Set Boundaries: Lay out limits with companions and friends in regards to ways of managing money and monetary conversations. Be confident in imparting your limits and stick to them, regardless of whether it implies expressing no to specific exercises or buys.

3. Find Similar Friends: Encircle yourself with companions who share comparable qualities and monetary objectives. Search out strong companionships where you can urge each other to settle on dependable decisions and oppose peer pressure together.

4. Practice Assertiveness: Figure out how to self-assuredly offer your viewpoints and inclinations without surrendering to peer pressure. Work on saying no cordially except for solidly when confronted with solicitations or ideas that conflict with your qualities or spending plan.

5. Offer Elective Suggestions: When companions propose costly or incautious exercises, recommend elective, spending plan amicable choices that actually consider mingling and having a good time. Support imaginative, minimal expense exercises that line up with your monetary objectives.

6. Be Positive about Your Choices: Pay attention to your gut feelings and be positive about your capacity to settle on autonomous choices. Recollect that it's OK to appear as something else and focus on your monetary prosperity over finding a place with peer assumptions.

7. Seek Backing in the event that Needed: Assuming you're battling to oppose peer pressure or oversee drive purchasing propensities, feel free to help from confided in grown-ups, like guardians, educators, or advisors. They can offer direction, support, and viable procedures to assist you with exploring peer communications and monetary difficulties.

8. Use Money Envelopes: Think about involving the money envelope framework for optional spending. Distribute a specific measure of money for each spending class (e.g., diversion, feasting out) and just use cash from the assigned envelopes for those costs. This visual and unmistakable technique can assist you with adhering to your financial plan and abstain from overspending.

9. Practice Careful Consumption:
Prior to making a buy, inquire as to whether the thing lines up with your qualities, fills a reasonable need, and gives certified pleasure or fulfillment. Practice careful utilization by zeroing in on higher expectations without compromise and putting resources into things that add to your prosperity and long haul joy.

10. Unsubscribe from Promoting Emails:
Lessen openness to allurement by withdrawing from promoting messages and warnings from retailers. Restricting your openness to limited time messages diminishes the probability of hasty purchases set off by deals and limits.

11. Find Free or Minimal expense Activities:
Investigate free or minimal expense exercises and side interests that give diversion and satisfaction without the requirement for burning through cash. Participate in outside exercises, humanitarian effort, imaginative pursuits, or local area occasions that line up with your inclinations and values.

12. Practice Positive Self-Talk:
Foster positive self-talk procedures to help certainty and strength in opposing companion pressure. Help

yourself to remember your assets, values, and objectives, and avow your capacity to settle on free decisions that line up with your needs.

13. Seek Job Models:
Distinguish positive good examples who exhibit dependable monetary propensities and decisive relational abilities. Gain from their encounters and look for direction on the best way to explore peer pressure and monetary difficulties actually.

14. Set Clear Monetary Goals:
Lay out clear monetary objectives and achievements that propel you to remain fixed on your needs. Whether it's putting something aside for a future buy, fabricating a backup stash, or contributing as long as possible, having unmistakable objectives assists you with opposing momentary enticements and remaining focused on your monetary arrangement.

15. Practice Saying No:
Pretend situations with companions or relatives where you work on expressing no to peer strain in a deferential and emphatic way. By practicing reactions and building trust in saying no, you'll be better prepared to deal with comparable circumstances, in actuality.

CHAPTER 5 CREDIT AND DEBT

Demystifying Credit: The Good, The Bad, and The Ugly

Credit is a strong monetary instrument that can open ways to valuable open doors and upgrade your personal satisfaction, however it likewise accompanies dangers and obligations. Understanding how credit functions, its advantages, downsides, and how potential traps are fundamental for pursuing informed monetary choices and building a strong monetary future. In this far reaching guide, we'll demystify credit by investigating its different angles

The Good: Advantages of Credit

1. Access to Financing: One of the essential advantages of credit is admittance to supporting significant guys like homes, vehicles, and instruction. Credit permits you to fan out the expense of these costs over the long run, making them more reasonable and sensible.

2. Building Credit History: Utilizing credit mindfully and making convenient installments assists you with laying out a positive record. A solid record is fundamental for fitting the bill for future advances, home loans, and Mastercards at positive terms and financing costs.

3. Emergency Asset Backup: Approaching acknowledgement can act as a wellbeing net during crises when you really want prompt assets however don't have adequate investment funds. Mastercards or credit extensions can give brief help until you can recharge your reserve funds.

4. Convenience and Flexibility: Mastercards offer accommodation and adaptability for ordinary exchanges, online buys, and travel costs. They kill the need to convey enormous amounts of money and give added security and extortion insurance.

5. Rewards and Perks: Many Visas offer prizes programs, cashback impetuses, and travel advantages for cardholders. By involving credit mindfully and taking care of balances in full every month, you can exploit these compensations to procure focuses, miles, or money back on your buys.

The Terrible: Downsides of Credit

1. Accumulating Debt: The simple entry to credit can prompt overspending and gathering obligation in the event that is not overseen mindfully. Conveying adjustments on Mastercards or credits can bring about exorbitant interest charges and long haul monetary pressure.

2. Interest Charges: Getting cash through acknowledgement comes for revenue charges, which can include essentially over the long run, particularly in the event that you just make least installments. Exorbitant loan fees on Visas can bring about paying considerably more for buys than their unique expense.

3. Credit Score Impact: Late installments, defaults, and high credit usage can adversely affect your FICO assessment, making it harder to meet all requirements for credits or credit from now on. An unfortunate financial assessment can likewise bring about higher loan fees and less ideal terms.

4. Hidden Charges and Penalties: Acknowledge arrangements frequently come for buried expenses, punishments, and fine print that borrowers may not completely comprehend. These charges can incorporate yearly expenses, balance move charges, late installment expenses, and punishment APRs, adding to the expense of acquiring.

5. Over Reliance on Credit: Depending too intensely on layaway to fund buys can make a pattern of reliance and sustain a way of life too far in the red. Finding some kind of harmony between utilizing credit capably and living inside your means is fundamental.

The Ugly: Traps of Credit Blunder

1. Debt Spiral: Blundering credit can prompt an obligation winding, where mounting obligation adjusts and exorbitant interest charges become progressively hard to reimburse. This cycle can bring about monetary difficulty, stress, and even liquidation in extreme cases.

2. Credit Card Fraud: Utilizing Mastercards for online exchanges or at new traders conveys the gamble of Visa misrepresentation and fraud.

Unapproved charges and false exercises can harm your FICO rating and undermine your monetary security.

3. Predatory Lending Practices: A few banks participate in ruthless loaning works on, focusing on weak purchasers with exorbitant loans, stowed away charges, and misleading terms. These practices can trap borrowers in patterns of obligation and compound monetary weaknesses.

4. Credit Score Damage: Defaulting on advances, bowing out of all financial obligations, or falling behind on installments can have enduring ramifications for your FICO assessment. A harmed FICO rating can frustrate your capacity to meet all requirements for credits, lease a condo, or even secure work.

5. Stress and Anxiety: Managing overpowering obligation and monetary weakness can negatively affect your psychological and close to home prosperity. Stress, uneasiness, and gloom are normal outcomes of credit fumble and monetary battles.

Credit is a situation with two sides that offers the two valuable open doors and dangers, relying upon how is made due. By figuring out the general mishmash parts of credit, you can arrive at informed conclusions about when and how to astutely utilize credit. Building a positive record as a consumer, keeping away from extreme obligation, and pursuing capable getting routines are fundamental for bridling the advantages of credit while relieving its downsides. With information, discipline, and cautious preparation, you can use credit to accomplish your monetary objectives and secure a more brilliant monetary future.

Managing Debt Wisely: Avoiding The Pitfall of Overspending

Obligation can be a helpful device when overseen carefully, however it can likewise turn into a critical weight in the event that is not dealt with as expected. For teenagers, understanding how to oversee obligation successfully is pivotal to laying out serious areas of strength for an establishment and staying away from the traps of exorbitant spending. Here is a broad aide on overseeing obligation admirably, with interesting models and viable guidance for adolescents.

Figuring out Debt

Obligation is cash acquired that should be reimbursed with revenue. Normal kinds of obligation incorporate understudy loans, Mastercard obligation, individual credits, and vehicle advances. While obligation can empower you to accomplish objectives like advanced education or purchasing a vehicle, it requires cautious administration to stay away from monetary pressure.

Standards of Overseeing Debt Admirably

1. Know Your Limits

Understanding your acquiring limit is the initial step to overseeing debt shrewdly. Since you're qualified for a credit or a Mastercard doesn't mean you ought to maximize it.

Model for Teens: In the event that you make some part-memories work and procure $300 every month, try not to get beyond what you can reimburse serenely. Assuming you're offered a Mastercard with a $1,000 limit, recall that your month to month pay restricts your capacity to rapidly take care of enormous equilibriums.

2. Borrow Just What You Need

Getting just what you really want forestalls pointless obligation aggregation. Try not to assume obligation for insignificant buys.

Model for Teens: Assuming you're putting something aside for a PC for school, work out the amount you want and get just that sum. Try not to involve credit for things like the most recent computer game control center or stylish garments that aren't fundamental.

3. Understand Loan fees and Terms

Prior to assuming obligation, comprehend the loan fees and reimbursement terms. Higher loan costs mean you'll pay more over the long run, so search for low-interest choices whenever the situation allows.

Model for Teens: In the event that you're thinking about a Mastercard, contrast cards and different loan costs. A card with a 15% loan fee will cost you less in revenue installments than one with a 25% rate, expecting you convey an equilibrium.

Viable Ways to oversee Debt
1. Create a Budget

A spending plan assists you with following your pay and costs, guaranteeing you can meet your obligation commitments without overspending.

Model for Teens: In the event that you procure $300 per month and have a $50 month to month telephone bill and $30 in different costs, you'll have $220 left. Plan to involve part of this for reserve funds and designate a particular sum for obligation reimbursement.

2. Pay More Than the Minimum

Assuming you just compensate the base sum due on your Debt, it will take more time to take care of and set you back more in interest. Paying more than the base speeds up Debt reimbursement and sets aside cash.

Model for Teens: On the off chance that you owe $500 on a charge card with a base installment of $25, paying $50 or more every month will pay off your obligation quicker and decline the interest you'll pay.

3. Avoid Drive Purchases

Drive buys can rapidly add to your obligation trouble. Consider cautiously about each buy and inquire as to whether it's vital or then again on the off chance that you can pause.

Model for Teens: In the event that you're enticed to purchase another set of tennis shoes spontaneously, require a day to thoroughly consider it. In the event that it's not fundamental, think about setting aside that cash or utilizing it to settle existing obligations.

4. Use Debt for Ventures, Not Consumables

Obligation ought to preferably be utilized for speculations that can build your future acquiring potential, like instruction, as opposed to consumables that don't offer long haul benefits.

Model for Teens: Utilizing an understudy loan to pay for school can be a wise interest in your future. Interestingly, utilizing a charge card to purchase costly contraptions that lose esteem rapidly is definitely not an insightful utilization of obligation.

Keeping away from Normal Traps

1. Peer Tension and Social Spending

Peer tension can prompt superfluous spending as you attempt to stay aware of companions. Adhere to your spending plan and monetary objectives, regardless of whether it implies saying no occasionally.

Model for Teens: If your companions have any desire to go out for a costly feast and it's not in your spending plan, propose a more reasonable other option or make sense of that you're putting something aside for something significant.

2. Falling for "Purchase Presently, Pay Later" Offers

"Purchase currently, pay later" plans can be enticing, yet they frequently lead to overspending and gathering obligations you might battle to reimburse.

Model for Teens: Assuming you're not kidding "purchase currently, pay later" choice for another telephone, recall that you'll in any case need to address the full cost ultimately, conceivably with added interest.

Consider setting aside and purchasing the telephone altogether all things considered.

3. Ignoring Bills and Payments
Overlooking bills or missing installments can prompt late charges, higher financing costs, and harm amazingly score. Keep steady over your installments to stay away from these issues.

Model for Teens: Set updates for installment due dates or mechanize installments to guarantee you never miss a cutoff time. This propensity will assist you with keeping a decent record as a consumer.

Building Solid Monetary Propensities

1. Set Monetary Goals
Defining clear monetary objectives assists you with keeping on track and persuading. Whether it's putting something aside for school, a vehicle, or an outing, having an objective provides motivation to your investment funds and spending choices.

Model for Teens: If you have any desire to save $1,000 for a mid year trip, separate it into month to month reserve funds objectives. On the off chance that you save $100 every month, you'll arrive at your objective in ten months.

2. Educate Yourself
Grasping monetary ideas and remaining informed about individual budgets can enable you to pursue better choices.

Model for Teens: Take an individual budget course, read books, or follow trustworthy monetary online journals to find out about planning, saving, money management, and obligation to the board.

3. Seek Counsel When Needed
Go ahead and exhortation from confided in grown-ups, monetary guides, or credit advisors in the event that you're uncertain about overseeing obligation or settling on monetary choices.

Model for Teens: In the event that you're thinking about taking out an understudy loan, examine the terms and suggestions with a parent or monetary counsel to guarantee you comprehend the responsibility and how it squeezes into your tentative arrangements.

Overseeing obligation shrewdly is tied in with pursuing informed decisions, defining limits, and keeping up with command over your funds. By knowing your cutoff points, getting mindfully, making a financial plan, and staying away from normal entanglements, you can involve obligation as an instrument to accomplish your objectives without falling into the snare of inordinate spending. Building these propensities from the beginning will show you a way to monetary security and achievement, assisting you explore the intricacies of individual budgets with no sweat.

CHAPTER 6: PLANNING FOR THE FUTURE

Exploring Higher Education: Financial Consideration For College

Deciding to seek after advanced education is perhaps one of the main choices you can make as a high schooler. While school can give significant open doors to individual and expert development, it additionally accompanies significant monetary ramifications. Understanding these monetary contemplations can assist you with pursuing informed choices, limit obligation, and amplify the profit from your interest in schooling. Here is a thorough aide on what to consider monetarily while investigating advanced education.

Figuring out the Expenses

The most vital phase in settling on informed monetary conclusions about school is understanding the different expenses included. These include:

1. Tuition and Fees: Educational cost is the expense of going to classes and can change broadly relying upon the foundation. Public schools and colleges frequently have lower educational cost rates for in-state understudies contrasted with out-of-state understudies or confidential foundations.

2. Room and Board: On the off chance that you intend to live nearby, food and lodging will cover lodging and feast plans. Off-grounds living can once in a while be less expensive, however it incorporates lease, utilities, and food costs that you'll have to plan for.

3. Books and Supplies: Course books and other required materials can add up rapidly. Utilized or computerized reading material and rentals are in many cases less expensive options in contrast to purchasing new ones.

4. Transportation: Whether you're driving from home or heading out to far off grounds, transportation expenses like gas, public travel, or flights can be huge.

5. Personal Expenses: Individual costs incorporate things like toiletries, amusement, and other everyday living expenses.

Wellsprings of Subsidizing
To deal with these expenses, investigating different wellsprings of funding is fundamental:

1. Scholarships
Grants are monetary honors that needn't bother with being reimbursed and are much of the time in view of legitimacy, ability, or explicit models like scholastic accomplishments, athletic abilities, or local area administration.

Model for Teens: Exploration and apply for grants early and frequently. Sites like Fastweb, Scholarships.com, and the School Board Grant Search can assist you with tracking down grants that match your profile. Nearby people group associations, organizations, and your secondary school direction office can likewise be significant assets.

2. Grants

Awards, similar to grants, needn't bother with being reimbursed and are generally founded on monetary need. The most notable award is the Government Pell Award, however many states and foundations offer awards too.

Model for Teens: Complete the Free Application for Government Understudy Help (FAFSA) as quickly as time permits. This structure decides your qualification for government awards, advances, and work-concentrate on programs, and numerous universities use it to grant their own monetary guide.

3. Student Loans

Understudy loans are acquired assets that should be reimbursed with interest. There are government and confidential understudy loans, each with various agreements.

Model for Teens: Government understudy loans regularly offer lower financing costs and more adaptable reimbursement choices than private credits. On the off chance that you really want to acquire, focus on government credits and get just what you really want. Comprehend the terms, loan costs, and reimbursement choices prior to committing.

4. Work-Study Programs

Work-concentrate on programs give temporary positions to understudies with monetary need, permitting them to bring in cash to help pay for school costs.

Model for Teens: Check assuming your school offers work-concentrate on open doors and go after jobs that line up with your timetable and scholarly responsibilities. These positions are many times nearby and can give important work insight.

Planning for School

Making a financial plan assists you with dealing with your cash successfully and keeping away from pointless obligations. This is the way to construct a financial plan for school:

1. Estimate Your Income

Work out your all out pay, including monetary guide, grants, awards, temporary work income, and any commitments from family.

Model for Teens: On the off chance that you get a $5,000 grant, a $3,000 Pell Award, and want to procure $2,000 from temporary work, your assessed yearly pay would be $10,000.

2. List Your Expenses

Recognize every one of your costs, including educational cost, food and lodging, books, transportation, and individual costs. Separate fixed costs e.g., educational cost from variable expenses e.g., diversion

Model for Teens: Fixed expenses could incorporate $15,000 for educational costs and charges, $10,000 for food and lodging, and $1,200 for books. Variable expenses could incorporate $200 each month for individual costs and $50 each month for transportation.

3. Compare Pay and Expenses
Contrast your complete assessed pay with your absolute costs. On the off chance that your costs surpass your pay, search for ways of decreasing expenses or increment pay.
Model for Teens: In the event that your all out costs are $30,000 and your pay is $10,000, you'll have to cover a $20,000 hole. Investigate extra grants, awards, or temporary work open doors, and consider cost-saving estimates like residing at home or going to a junior college for the initial two years.

4. Adjust Your Budget
Change your financial plan depending on the situation over time. Monitor your spending and make changes assuming you find you're overspending in specific regions.
Model for Teens: Assuming you notice you're spending more on eating out than you planned, consider preparing more dinners at home or utilizing grounds feasting choices to set aside cash.

Cost-Saving Methodologies
To additionally oversee school costs, think about these methodologies:

1. Attend Junior college First
Beginning at a junior college and afterward moving to a four-year establishment can essentially diminish the expense of a four year college education.
Model for Teens: Junior colleges frequently have lower educational cost rates, and many have moved concurrently with four-year colleges. Finishing your overall instruction

prerequisites at a junior college can save a great many dollars.

2. Live at Home
Residing at home while going to school can get a good deal on food and lodging. This choice isn't doable for everybody, except it tends to be a significant expense saving measure.

Model for Teens: In the event that your school is within driving distance, think about residing at home and driving to grounds. The investment funds on lodging and feast plans can be critical.

3. Buy Utilized or Advanced Textbooks
Course readings can be a massive cost. Search for utilized or advanced variants, or lease course readings to set aside cash.

Model for Teens: Sites like Chegg, Amazon, and your ground book shop frequently offer utilized course readings or rental choices for a portion of the expense of new books.

4. Limit Eating Out and Entertainment
While mingling is a significant piece of the school insight, successive eating out and diversion can rapidly deplete your spending plan.

Model for Teens: Select free or minimal expense exercises like grounds occasions, joining clubs, or facilitating film evenings. Use understudy limits and search for neighborhood arrangements to take full advantage of your amusement spending plan.

Anticipating What's to come
Figuring long haul about your funds can assist you with settling on better

choices today. Think about the accompanying:

1. Understand Your Vocation Prospects

Research the procuring potential and occupation viewpoint for your picked field of study. A few professions require postgraduate education and have high procuring potential, while others may not legitimize critical understudy loan obligation.

Model for Teens: In the event that you're thinking about a vocation in designing, research the typical beginning compensations and occupation situation rates for graduates in your field. This data can assist you with concluding how much obligation is sensible to take on for your schooling.

2. Develop a Reimbursement Plan

On the off chance that you take out educational loans, make a reimbursement plan before you graduate. Comprehend your advance terms, reimbursement choices, and methodologies for taking care of obligations rapidly.

Model for Teens: Government understudy loans offer different reimbursement plans, including pay driven choices. Research these plans and pick one that accommodates what is going on after graduation.

3. Build a Crisis Fund

Having a backup stash can assist you with overseeing startling costs without depending on Mastercards or extra advances. Intend to save a modest quantity every month to fabricate a pad after some time.

Model for Teens: In any event, saving $20 a month can accumulate over the long haul. Utilize a high return investment account to procure revenue on your secret stash. Investigating advanced education includes huge monetary preparation and navigation. By figuring out the expenses, investigating different money sources, making a financial plan, and carrying out cost-saving procedures, you can deal with your school expenses really
. Making arrangements for your monetary future, exploring professional prospects, and fostering a reimbursement plan are urgent moves toward guaranteeing that your interest in training pays off. With cautious preparation and brilliant monetary decisions, you can explore the intricacies of paying for school and put yourself positioned for long haul monetary achievement.

Looking Ahead: Building a Financially Secure Future

As a teen, the prospect of building a Financially secure future might appear to be far off or in any event, overpowering. Notwithstanding, beginning early is perhaps the best choice you can make for your monetary prosperity. Growing great monetary propensities presently can prepare for a steady and prosperous future. This guide will give broad experiences into steps you can take as a high schooler to get your monetary future.
Figuring out Financial Security

Financial security implies having an adequate number of assets to meet your current and future necessities, being ready for crises, and having the opportunity to seek after your objectives without unnecessary worry about cash. It incorporates saving, effective money management, planning, and making arrangements for long haul objectives.

Growing Great Financial Propensities

1. Start Saving Early

The earlier you begin saving, the more you can profit from building interest. Indeed, even modest quantities saved consistently can develop fundamentally over the long run.

Model for Teens: On the off chance that you save $50 a month beginning at age 15, and it procures a typical yearly financing cost of 5%, you could have more than $4,000 when you turn 21. The influence of progressive accrual brings in your cash quicker.

2. Set Monetary Goals

Having clear, feasible monetary objectives assists you with remaining persuaded and centered. Objectives can be present moment (putting something aside for another telephone), medium-term (putting something aside for school), or long haul (fabricating a retirement store).

Model for Teens: Record your financial objectives and the means you want to take to accomplish them. For example, to save $600 for a PC, decide the amount you really want to save every month and keep tabs on your development.

3. Create a Budget

A spending plan assists you with following your pay and costs, guaranteeing you live inside your means and save for your objectives. It's a basic device for financial preparation.

Model for Teens: In the event that you procure $200 per month from temporary work, make a financial plan that designates cash for reserve funds, spending, and any bills you have. For example, you could choose to save $50, burn through $100 on private costs, and keep $50 for surprising expenses.

Finding out About Cash The board
1. Educate Yourself

Understanding monetary ideas like loan fees, financial assessments, and contributing can assist you with pursuing informed choices. There are numerous assets accessible, including books, online courses, and monetary proficiency programs.

Model for Teens: Read books like "Rich Father Unfortunate Father" by Robert Kiyosaki or "The High Schooler's Manual for Individual Budget" by Joshua Holmberg. Sites like Investopedia offer articles and instructional exercises on different monetary subjects.

2. Open a Bank Account

Having a ledger shows you how to oversee cash and acquaints you with banking administrations. Begin with an investment account and consider financial records when you're prepared.

Model for Teens: Request that your folks assist you with opening a bank account at a neighborhood bank or credit association. Use it to store your income and watch your investment funds develop.

3. Learn to Utilize Credit Wisely

Credit can be a valuable device whenever oversaw mindfully. Comprehend how credit functions, including Mastercards, loan fees, and the significance of keeping a decent FICO rating.

Model for Teens: Assuming that your folks concur, you could turn into an approved client on their Visa. This can assist you with figuring out how to utilize credit capably while building your financial record.

Making arrangements for What's in store

1. Consider Advanced education Costs

School can be a huge cost, yet there are ways of dealing with these expenses, including grants, awards, seasonal positions, and understudy loans. Begin investigating and arranging early.

Model for Teens: Utilize online apparatuses like the FAFSA4caster to gauge your qualification for government understudy help. Search for grants and awards in your field of interest, and consider beginning a school investment funds reserve.

2. Start Investing

Contributing is a strong method for creating financial stability over the long run. Find out about various sorts of speculations, like stocks, securities, and common assets, and think about beginning with modest quantities.

Model for Teens: Use applications like Oak seeds or Robinhood, which are easy to use for fledglings. Begin with little ventures and step by step as you become more agreeable and learned.

3. Think About Retirement Early

While retirement might appear to be quite far off, beginning to save early can have an enormous effect. Accumulate interest can fundamentally build your retirement investment funds over the long haul.

Model for Teens: In the event that you have some work, think about opening a Roth IRA. Commitments are made with after-charge cash, yet your withdrawals in retirement are tax-exempt.

Safeguarding Your Financial Future

1. Build a Crisis Fund

A secret stash is cash saved to cover startling costs, for example, vehicle fixes or doctor's visit expenses. Plan to save three to a half year of everyday costs.

Model for Teens: Start just barely every month, for example, $20. Over the long haul, this asset will develop and give a monetary pad to crises.

2. Avoid Obligation Traps

Acquiring cash can be fundamental now and again, however it's critical to keep away from exorbitant premium obligations and getting beyond what you can stand to reimburse.

Model for Teens: Use Mastercards capably by taking care of the equilibrium every month to stay away from interest charges. Stay away from payday advances and other exorbitant interest acquiring choices.

3. Understand Insurance

Protection safeguards you from monetary misfortune because of mishaps, medical problems, or other startling occasions. Find out about various kinds of protection and how they work.

Model for Teens: On the off chance that you're driving, guarantee you have vehicle protection. As you progress in years and begin working, investigate health care coverage and other applicable arrangements.

Looking for Direction and Backing

1. Talk to Guardians and Mentors

Your folks and other believed grown-ups can give significant guidance and offer their monetary encounters. Go ahead and for direction.

Model for Teens: Talk about your monetary objectives and plans with your folks. They can offer bits of knowledge and assist you with keeping away from normal slip-ups.

2. Utilize School Resources

Many schools offer monetary proficiency courses or then again have advocates who can give exhortation on monetary preparation and school financing. Exploit these assets to improve your monetary information.

Model for Teens: Sign up for any suitable individual budget or financial aspects classes at your school. Meet with your life coach to talk about school subsidizing choices and grant valuable open doors.

3. Seek Proficient Advice

As you age, consider talking with a monetary counselor for customized guidance custom-made to your objectives and monetary circumstance.

Model for Teens: When you start your most memorable everyday work, plan a gathering with a monetary consultant to examine long haul reserve funds systems, venture choices, and retirement arranging.

Building Monetary Flexibility

1. Develop a Development Mindset

Embrace a development outlook by reviewing monetary moves as any open doors to learn and develop. Remain open to new data and consistently try to work on your monetary abilities.

Model for Teens: In the event that you commit a monetary error, for example, overspending, break down what turned out badly and how you can stay away from comparative issues from now on. Utilize each insight as learning an open door.

2. Stay Informed About Monetary Trends

The monetary world is continually advancing, with recent fads, innovations, and valuable open doors arising. Remaining informed can assist you with settling on better choices and adjusting to changes.

Model for Teens: Follow monetary news sites, buy into finance-related bulletins, and join online networks where you can talk about monetary themes with peers.

3. Practice Discipline and Patience

Building monetary security takes time and requires discipline and persistence. Keep away from the compulsion to pursue speedy gains or settle on indiscreet monetary choices.

Model for Teens: Put forth a drawn out reserve funds objective and stick to it, regardless of whether it implies making momentary penances. For instance, putting something aside for a drawn out movement experience after secondary school can be a remunerating long haul objective that requires trained saving and spending.

Embracing Monetary Obligation

1. Understand the Worth of Money

Perceive that cash is a device that can assist you with accomplishing your objectives, however it requires dependable administration. Value the work it takes to bring in cash and spend it shrewdly.

Model so that Teens: Track your spending for a month to see where your cash goes. Recognize regions where you can scale back and divert those assets towards reserve funds or speculations.

2. Foster a Reserve funds Culture

Foster a propensity for saving a piece of any cash you get, whether it's from a stipend, a temporary work, or gifts. Developing an investment funds culture from the beginning can prompt significant monetary development over the long haul.

Model for Teens: Take on the "pay yourself first" rule by saving a level of your income for reserve funds prior to spending on different things. Mean to save something like 10% of your pay.

3. Promote Monetary Education Among Peers

Share your insight about monetary administration with companions and urge them to embrace great monetary propensities. Aggregate monetary

education can prompt better monetary choices inside your group of friends.
Model for Teens: Coordinate a monetary education club at school where you and your companions can examine themes like planning, money management, and saving. Sharing information can engage everybody to settle on better monetary decisions. Building a Financially secure future as a high schooler is tied in with settling on informed decisions, growing great monetary propensities, and remaining focused on your objectives. By beginning early, setting clear monetary targets, instructing yourself about cash the executives,

CONCLUSION

Empowering Teens for Financial Independence

In "Teen Financial Guide: Money Wisdom for Modern Living," we've embarked on a journey to empower teens with the knowledge, skills, and mindset needed to navigate the complex world of personal finance. From understanding the importance of financial literacy to mastering the art of budgeting, saving, and investing, this book has provided comprehensive guidance for teens to build a solid financial foundation.

Throughout these pages, we've explored the principles of wise money management, emphasizing the significance of starting early, setting clear goals, and making informed financial decisions. We've delved into topics such as managing debt, exploring job opportunities, and making smart purchasing choices, equipping teens with practical strategies to avoid common financial pitfalls and achieve financial independence.

As we conclude this journey, it's essential to remember that financial success is not just about accumulating wealth but also about living a life of purpose, fulfillment, and security. By embracing the principles outlined in this book, teens have the opportunity to take control of their financial futures, overcome challenges, and pursue their dreams with confidence. Whether it's planning for higher education, building an emergency fund, or investing for the future, the principles of financial literacy and responsibility laid out in this guide will serve as valuable tools for teens as they navigate the journey to adulthood.

As you close the pages of "Teen Financial Guide," remember that the power to shape your financial destiny lies within you. By applying the knowledge and wisdom gained from this book, you have the opportunity to embark on a journey towards a brighter, and more prosperous future. Cheers to your financial success, empowerment, and resilience. May you navigate life's financial challenges

with grace, wisdom, and determination, and may your journey towards financial freedom be filled with abundance, growth, and fulfillment.
Warm regards,
Richard R. Montemayor

www.ingramcontent.com/pod-product-compliance
Lightning Source LLC
Chambersburg PA
CBHW050235230526
45470CB00005B/1964